Farm Animals

Pigs

Rachael Bell

Heinemann Library
Chicago, Illinois

Customer Service 888-454-2279

Designed by AMR
Originated by Ambassador Litho
Printed in China

07 06
10 9 8 7 6 5 4

Library of Congress Cataloging-in-Publication Data
Bell, Rachael.
    Pigs / Rachael Bell.
        p. cm. – (Farm animals)
    Includes bibliographical references (p.) and index.
    Summary: Introduces this familiar farm animal by describing its physical appearance, manner of reproduction, eating and sleeping habits, ways of staying healthy, required care, and uses.
    ISBN 1-57572-532-0 (lib. bdg.)   ISBN 1-58810-366-8 (pbk. bdg.)
    1. Swine—Juvenile literature. [1. Pigs.] I. Title.
    SF395.5B46 2000
    636.4—dc21   99-043371
                                                                    CIP

Acknowledgments
The Publishers would like to thank the following for permission to reproduce photographs:
Agripicture/Peter Dean, p. 6; Farmers Weekly Picture Library, pp. 8, 13, 18, 20; Garden Matters/John Phipps, pp. 12, 16; Holt Studios/Sarah Rowland, pp. 4 (top), 14, 28 (bottom); Holt Studios/Nigel Cattlin, p. 4 (bottom),10, 11, & 24; Holt Studios/Gordon Roberts, p.25; Chris Honeywell, pp. 22, 27; Images of Nature/FLPA/Silvestris, p. 5; Images of Nature/FLPA/E. & D. Hosking, p. 9; Images of Nature/FLPA/J. C. Allen, p. 15; Images of Nature/FLPA/Peter Dean, p. 17; Images of Nature/FLPA/M. Nimmo, p. 26; NHPA/B. A. Janes, p. 19; D. B. Pineider, p. 23; Lynn M. Stone, p. 28 (top); Tony Stone Images/H. Richard Johnston, p. 7; Tony Stone Images/ Andy Sacks, p. 21.

Cover photograph reproduced with permission of Farmers Weekly Picture Library.

Our thanks to the American Farm Bureau Federation for their comments in the preparation of this book.

Some words are shown in bold, **like this.** You can find out what they mean by looking in the glossary.

636.4 B

Contents

Pig Relatives

Farmers all over the world **raise** pigs.
Farm pigs have short, **bristly** hair.
There are many different **breeds**
of pigs.

There are wild pigs in many parts of the world. These are wild **boars.** They are smaller than farm pigs. They also have more hair.

Welcome to the Farm

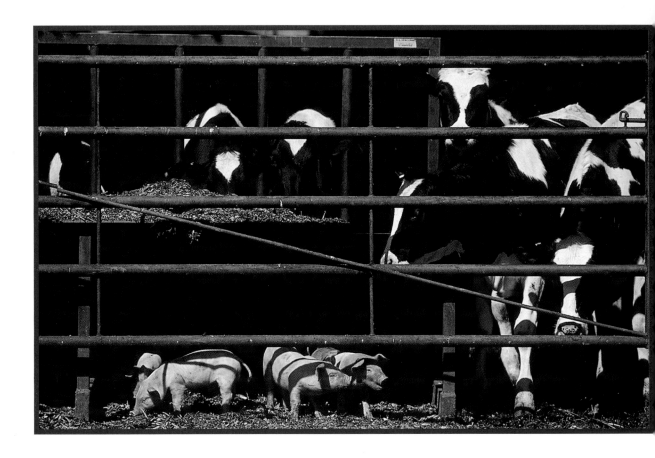

Farmers often **raise** more than one kind of animal on their farms. On this farm, there are pigs and cows.

Some of the land is used to grow wheat,
barley, or corn. Some of it is **milled**
and fed to the pigs.

Meet the Pigs

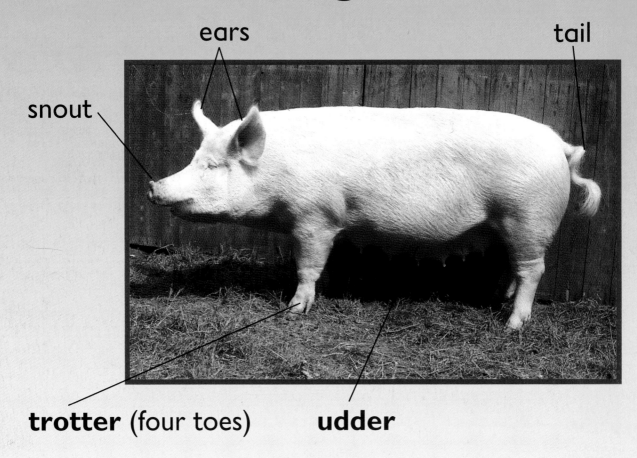

ears

tail

snout

trotter (four toes)

udder

Female pigs are called sows. Sows eat a lot. An adult pig can weigh as much as a piano!

tusk

Male pigs are called **boars**. Some males have **tusks**. They use the tusks for digging and for fighting other pigs.

Meet the Baby Pigs

Baby pigs are called piglets. A newborn piglet weighs about as much as a bag of sugar. Piglets can walk soon after they are born.

Sows usually have about eleven piglets in each **litter**. The piglets get milk from their mother. The sow grunts to call them to feed from her.

Where Do Pigs Live?

On some farms, the pigs live in indoor **pens**. They have straw **bedding** to keep them clean and warm. The farmer changes the straw every two days.

The pigs lie in one part of the pen that is warm and dry. They get up to eat in a different part of the pen. There is a feed **trough** and a **waterer**.

What Do Pigs Eat?

Adult pigs can eat almost anything. But most pig food is made from **grain**. Farmers are careful to give their pigs food that is good for them.

Piglets get milk from their mother until they are about three weeks old. Then they eat special **pellets**. Older pigs eat liquid food, like thick soup.

Staying Healthy

Piglets play-fight almost as soon as they are born. This is good exercise. It keeps them fit.

Pigs like to **wallow** in wet mud or straw. This keeps them cool in hot weather. The mud keeps the pigs' skin safe from the sun.

How Do Pigs Sleep?

When a pig sleeps alone, it usually lies on one side with its legs out straight. But pigs often sleep close to each other to keep warm.

Pigs spend a lot of time sleeping in nests they make in their straw. They wake up a few times to eat and drink. They are most **active** early in the morning and just before dark.

Raising Pigs

Sows can have more than one **litter** in a year. When the sow is about to have babies, the farmer may put her in a **pen** by herself.

The farmer has to be careful that the sow doesn't roll over on the piglets.

How Are Pigs Used?

The meat from pigs is called pork.
It is made into many different foods.
Sausage, bacon, and ham are all
made from pork.

Pigskin can be used to make purses, gloves, and wallets. Some brushes are made from pig **bristles**. Some baseball gloves are stuffed with hair from pigs.

Other Kinds of Pig Farms

On some pig farms, the pigs spend most of their time outside in open **lots**. There are small houses for **shelter**.

On large pig farms, pigs are kept in special buildings. The pigs grow very quickly indoors. The farmer can **raise** thousands of pigs at a time.

More Pig Farms

Some farmers **raise organic** pigs. This means that the pigs do not get any **additives** in their food. Most organic pigs live outside.

The meat from organic pigs usually costs more than ordinary pork. Many people think this kind of meat is better to eat.

Fact File

If you grew as quickly as a newborn piglet, you would double your weight every week!

Some sows have as many as 35 piglets in a year. Sows can only feed twelve piglets at once, so any extras have to be given to another sow to feed.

Pigs are also called hogs or swine.

Pigs have a very good sense of smell. In some countries, farmers train their pigs to smell out truffles. These are a kind of mushroom that grows underground.

 Farmers sometimes say that the only thing you cannot eat from a pig is its **squeal!** This is because people in many places cook and use every part of the pig—even the **trotters.**

Glossary

active awake and moving around

additive medicine or other substance put in animals' food to keep them healthy or make them grow

barley plant that can be made into cereal

bedding what pigs lie on

boar male or wild pig

breed group of animals with the same ancestors

bristle short, stiff hair

grain plant such as corn or wheat

litter group of animals born together from one mother

lot large, open area with a fence around it

milled ground up

organic grown without chemicals or sprays

pellet dry pig food that has been mixed and then pressed into one piece

pen small, fenced-in area for animals

raise to feed and take care of young animals or children

shelter place that gives protection from bad weather

snout nose and mouth of a pig

squeal noise a pig makes when it is excited or angry

trotter pig foot

trough long, open container that holds food for animals

tusk large tooth that grows up and out of the mouth of a pig

udder part of an animal's body where milk is stored

wallow to roll around or lie in something

waterer type of water fountain for animals

More Books to Read

Brady, Peter. *Pigs*. Danbury, Conn.: Children's Press, 1996.

Fowler, Allan. *Smart, Clean Pigs*. Danbury, Conn.: Children's Press, 1993.

Hansen, Ann L. *Pigs*. Minneapolis: ABDO Publishing Company, 1997.

Index